BISHOPSTONE
AND
SEAFORD
IN OLD PHOTOGRAPHS

ALL THE CHILDREN OF BISHOPSTONE SCHOOL, taken on the green in 1937. Back row, left to right: Toni Laughlin, Winnie Cox, Joan Warren, Harold Gutsell, Vera Warren, Lesley Young, Christine Pople, Kathleen Pilbeam, Eileen West, Jack Hammond, Aubrey White, ? Nolan, John Young, Alan Smith, Don Moore, Ivor Pilbeam, Denny Moore, –. Front row, left to right: Gladys Laughlin, Dick Dale, Joyce Standen, Alan Laughlin, -?-, Roger Smith, Iris Cox, Rose Geering, Muriel Alderson, Doreen Standen, Margaret Young, Jean Moore, David Westwood, Percy Cox, -?-.

BISHOPSTONE
AND
SEAFORD
IN OLD PHOTOGRAPHS

COLLECTED BY

PHILIP POPLE AND PATRICIA BERRY

ALAN SUTTON

Alan Sutton Publishing Limited
Phoenix Mill · Far Thrupp · Stroud · Gloucestershire

First Published 1991

British Library Cataloguing in Publication Data

Bishopstone and Seaford in old photographs.
I. Pople, Philip, *1953–*
II. Berry, Patricia, *1929–*
942.312

ISBN 0-86299-964-2

Typeset in 9/10 Korinna.
Typesetting and origination by
Alan Sutton Publishing Limited.
Printed in Great Britain by
The Bath Press, Avon.

CONTENTS

BISHOPSTONE   6

1.   BISHOPSTONE ROAD TO NORTON   9

2.   PEOPLE AND SOCIAL EVENTS   41

3.   FARMING   63

4.   LITTLE HALLANDS   71

5.   SNOW   81

SEAFORD   84

6.   COASTLINE   87

7.   STREETS   91

8.   SHOPS AND BUSINESSES   95

9.   BUILDINGS   101

10. PEOPLE   109

11. CHURCHES   117

12. EVENTS   121

13. SCHOOLS   127

14. MILITARY   135

15. STORMS, FLOODS AND WRECKS   139

16. PANORAMAS   145

17. TIDEMILLS   151

18   NEARBY   155

THIS IS THE CART THAT WAS USED by Louis Suitter to take the milk from Bishopstone to Kennard's Dairy in Seaford. The photograph was taken in around 1928 at the back of the Manor House.

BISHOPSTONE

The village of Bishopstone lies three-quarters of a mile from the busy Newhaven to Seaford road. Fortunately, even today it has retained much of its shy charm and seclusion described by the Revd James Hurdis in his great poem of 1800, *The Favourite Village.*

The name Bishopstone means Bishop's Manor; the manor belonged to the see of Chichester from the early eighth century until the sixteenth century. The Bishop appears to have resided here frequently, and its degree of importance can be judged by the fact that King Edward II was entertained here for two days in 1324.

In the fourteenth century Bishopstone gave Chichester Cathedral a chancellor, who took his name from his place of birth. Chancellor John Bishopstone by his will of 1324 left a chalice, twenty shillings and a cope 'to the Church of Bishopstone in which I was baptised.'

During the reign of Henry VIII the manor of Bishopstone was leased and came into the hands of the Pelham family some time during the sixteenth century. Their ownership of land at Bishopstone is first mentioned in the will of Sir John Pelham dated 1580. He left the manor to his son Oliver, and from him it passed to John's brother Thomas, who was created 1st Baronet by James I in 1611. The Pelhams constructed a house on the site of the Bishop's Manor, which in due course was used by Thomas Pelham, Duke of Newcastle, for hunting and for his lavish entertainment during the Seaford parliamentary elections.

The election of 1747 is rather interesting: one of the two candidates was William Pitt, later Earl of Chatham. On the eve of the election Pitt had been invited to dinner at Bishopstone, at which all the local farmers and other gentlemen were present. There followed an enormous feast which lasted all night, and at daybreak all were piled into carriages and driven to Seaford, to vote for the duke's candidate.

The duke died in November 1768. He was buried at Laughton, and above the main door of Bishopstone Place was hung his hatchment, which stayed in place for the next year and was then hung in the church, as was the tradition.

In 1772 the Pelhams tried to lease the house, and a description in the *Sussex Weekly Advertiser* of that time is worthy of mention. 'The house is strong and well built, not large, but has several good rooms in which there are many fine paintings of the Royal Family and the noble family, together with stabling for thirty horses, coach-house and gardens.' The estate, though, was held by Lord Pelham as lessee under the prebend of Chichester, and it was not until the early nineteenth century that the Pelhams had the estate outright.

The house was demolished in 1831 and all that remains today are a few walls, the cellars, and the old and new kitchen gardens, the latter dating from 1773. Both Bishopstone and Norton farms were used to supply the enormous demands of the Pelham mansion at Halland near Laughton.

The 1801 census gives Bishopstone a population of 188 and an acreage of 1,785. The parish of Bishopstone is bounded by the ancient King's Hedges on the south, Tidemills and the sea on the west as far as Cut Hole near Mount Pleasant, Five Lord Burgh on the north, and Cradle Valley to the east. Between the railway embankment and the A259 are the fields called Newlands. In the fields are two banks; these are possibly an early form of sea defence.

It would appear that from time to time the entire Bishopstone valley could be flooded with sea water; two such events are recorded. On 3 December 1794 the burial took place of one John Towner who had been clerk of the parish and sexton for forty years; it was John Towner's house that had been flooded with sea water some years earlier. This house must have been in the area where White Row Cottages now stand.

Another flood was in the year 1824 when incalculable damage was done by the breaking down of one of the principal dams by the sea. It was in this flood that a barge was washed up as far as Norton, the remains of which were visible until as late as the 1940s.

It was not only the land that was suffering from excess moisture at this time. At the foot of a letter in 1826 James Henry Hurdis refers to the dampness in the church and states that 'the roof is in many parts completely unroofed and it can only proceed from nothing else than total neglect.' These must have been some of the reasons for the first restoration of the church in 1849.

Although after 1831 the Pelhams no longer had a residence in the village, they still had the estate, this forming part of the Earl of Chichester's vast estates in

Sussex. Towards the end of the last century Bishopstone farm was sold to Mr Harry Willett, although Norton farm was not sold until the early years of this century. The Pelhams' last remaining link with the parish was the school. This had been given by the Earl of Chichester in 1849, and was vested in the vicar and churchwardens for such time as it remained a school. The school closed in 1944 and the building was sold by the heirs of the donor. It was purchased as a village hall in 1959 for £600.

During the 1930s most of Bishopstone was sold for development; the station was built, together with a few houses and bungalows in Hill Rise, Station Road, Bishopstone Road and Marine Drive. Luckily, all building ceased with the Second World War, the station and a lot of the bungalows being occupied by troops. It is interesting to note that in 1951 the population of the parish was 397.

During the 1950s the majority of the farm was bought back from the developers, with the exception of Hawth Hill, where building started in 1962, and Harbour View estate where building commenced in the late 1960s. Fortunately, no new houses have been built in the village since 1936, although most of the farm buildings have been converted sympathetically into dwellings. The fact that there has been no new building has made the place unique today, somewhere that must be carefully preserved for future generations.

The Bishopstone part of the book is in five sections, the first being from Bishopstone Road through the village and on to Norton. I have tried to include most buildings, where possible. Section Two includes people and social events; this entailed some very interesting evenings trying to sort out dates and names, but bear with me if some are incorrect, and please let me know. Thirdly we have farming and related subjects, fourthly Little Hallands at Norton, and lastly a few snow scenes. I hope that you find it interesting and enjoyable.

I am indeed grateful to all the people who have recalled their memories and anecdotes to me over many years, and to both my grandfathers' foresight in taking so many photographs of the parish over a period of fifty years.

I am also most grateful to the following people who have so kindly loaned me photographic material: Mr J. Carreck, Mr and Mrs J.F. Collinson, Mr G. Jakens, Mrs L. Ockenden, Mr C. Rose, Mrs N. Warrell, Mr G.J. White, Mr J.A. Willett, Mrs C. Woolmer.

Bishopstone Road to Norton

THE BISHOPSTONE ESTATE in around 1936, from the bottom of Hawth Hill. In 1934 nearly all of Bishopstone Farm was sold for development. This postcard shows the first bungalows in Bishopstone Road, Marine Drive and Rookery Way, the plots being 35 ft in width and 250 ft in depth, and ranging in price from £700 freehold.

BISHOPSTONE ROAD in around 1947, with four bungalows and two hay-stacks in Rookery Way. During the Second World War several bungalows were occupied by troops, and one Sunday afternoon bombs dropped in the area between Bishopstone Road and Rookery Way.

BISHOPSTONE ROAD FROM WAY FIELD. This was photographed in around 1957, with a few more bungalows in Rookery Way, and Newhaven in the distance.

TIDEMILLS FROM ROOKERY HILL. The field in the foreground is now the Harbour View Estate, and was photographed in 1952.

STUD FARM AND NEWHAVEN from Rookery Hill in 1952: how different from today's view.

BISHOPSTONE FROM ROOKERY HILL. This is a quite remarkable photograph, taken between 1900 and 1910. The walled manor garden can be clearly seen together with several of the cottages. The photograph must have been taken on a Monday judging by the amount of washing hanging out to dry, which looks like nightshirts or smocks.

THE POND AND BISHOPSTONE ROAD in around 1925 with Dog Kennel Barn in the distance. The church is hidden by the splendid elm trees in Lady's Meadow and by the group of trees known as the Twelve Apostles. This area was the park of Bishopstone Place.

BISHOPSTONE ROAD AND THE CHURCH OF ST ANDREW. This stretch of road was originally the drive of Bishopstone Place.

THE MANOR HOUSE. On the front of this fine building can be seen the Pelham buckle, the emblem of the Pelham family, with the initials T.P. for Thomas, 1st Baron Pelham of Laughton, and the date 1688. This was the steward or bailiff's house during the Pelhams' time, and was later occupied by the tenant farmers.

THE MANOR HOUSE in around 1905. This was the home successively of the Farncombe, Willett and Fowler families. In the 1930s it became a prep school run jointly by Miss Carpenter and Miss Warner. During the early years of the Second World War many British and Canadian troops were billeted here. Finally, in 1948 the house was divided into three well-proportioned residences.

DOG KENNEL BARN in around 1914. A fine view of the back of the Manor House, and also of the then vicarage and the road to Norton.

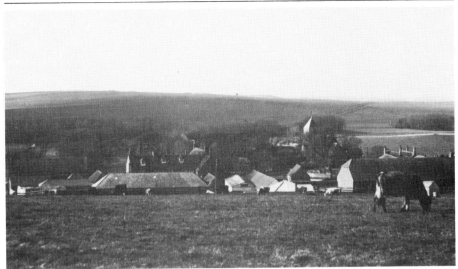

MANOR FARM FROM WHITEGATE FIELD, looking towards Rookery Hill. Nearly all the farm buildings here have now been converted into dwelling-houses, although the barn on the right was pulled down in the late 1960s.

BISHOPSTONE PLACE FROM THE SOUTH. This is the site of the Bishop's Manor and remained in the possession of the bishops until the early sixteenth century. It then came into the hands of the great Pelham family, who rebuilt the house as seen in this copy of a print. The house was demolished in 1831 and many of the bricks and building materials used in and around the parish.

A WATERCOLOUR OF THE CHURCH signed R.H.N. 1806. This shows a large Georgian window in the nave, a small window high up in the chancel, the original east window and two more buttresses to the sanctuary. All these features were swept away in the 1849 restoration.

ANOTHER WATERCOLOUR OF 1806, with the church and Bishopstone Place clearly visible. Summer Cottage is below the church. The row of cottages stood on the site of Post Office Cottages, which were thatched. They burned down in the middle of the last century.

THE PARISH CHURCH OF ST ANDREW photographed in around 1905. This is one of the oldest churches in Sussex, the Saxon porch being built some time between the sixth and ninth centuries. In the distance can be seen Bishopstone House, which was formerly the vicarage.

INTERIOR OF THE CHURCH in 1894. Above the alter is painted 'I am the bread of life'. The pulpit is the forerunner of the present one and the oil lamps are a charming reminder of the days before electricity.

THE ALTAR AND CHOIRSTALLS of the church, decorated for Easter. In the arches are painted the Lord's Prayer and the Ten Commandments.

THIS CHARMING VIEW OF THE CHURCH PORCH was taken in 1908. The doorway is Norman and shows the crisp detail of the carving; above is the Saxon sundial with the inscription 'Eadric'. The small girl is Ivy Simmonds, the four-year-old grand-daughter of Jasper and Sarah Simmonds of the Post Office.

THE EAST END OF THE CHURCH in around 1925. This end of the churchyard is almost entirely taken up with the tombs and vaults of the Cooper family from Norton and the Catt family from Tidemills. The railings were removed during the Second World War.

A VIEW OF THE DIARY AND YARD. This is now the very attractive garden of The Granary, Monks Down Barn and the dairy.

A POSTCARD OF SILVER LANE OR BLACKSMITH HOLLOW. On a May or June morning in around 1925, horse and hayrake begin the day's work.

FROM SILVER LANE looking towards Bishopstone House. In the foreground is the house known as Plummers and built by Mr George Hughes. George was one of a small group of dedicated people who did so much to preserve this area of downland from development.

NEW BARN AT HARVEST TIME and the village in the distance. All this area was sold as building land during the 1930s. After much discussion, the land again became part of Bishopstone Farm and is now protected within this Area of Outstanding Natural Beauty.

SILVER LANE. On the right of this photograph is the forge, which had been on this site since as early as 1530. Two horse-drawn rollers are being repaired outside the forge during the early twenties.

FORGE COTTAGES, Nos 121 and 122, and Monks Down Barn. This barn was used for the harvest suppers, and one can imagine much merriment there each autumn.

MONKS DOWN. This house was the home for many years of Mr W.A. Darlington, drama critic of the *Daily Telegraph*. The glass verandah just visible at the front of the house was brought down by enemy bombs on 15 May 1941.

CLEAVERS. Formerly known as Priory Cottage, it dates from the early seventeenth century. The name Cleavers refers to the family who lived there during the eighteenth and nineteenth centuries, and who lie buried in the churchyard.

SUMMER COTTAGE, No. 123. It is now called Copsford and has been much enlarged. This is quite an early building and was two-up and two-down, with a cellar as well.

THE VICARAGE. Built during the last century and called The Downs, it was given as a vicarage in the early 1930s by Sir Malcolm Fraser 1st Baronet. The servants' wing at the back was demolished in the 1970s. The back of Post Office Cottages, Nos 134 to 136, can be seen on the right.

THE OLD POST OFFICE. This photograph must have been taken during the early years of this century. The building was probably used as a store after the new post office was built opposite. Outside stands Mrs Simmonds.

AN EARLIER VIEW OF THE OLD POST OFFICE. As can be seen, this building came right to the edge of the road. Outside stands the mail or delivery cart.

A CLOSE-UP OF THE OLD POST OFFICE. The garage of Copsford now stands on this site. It was from here that James Hurdis must have posted his letters to the poet Cowper. From here, all mail was taken to meet the Seaford to Lewes mail cart at the end of Bishopstone Road. Most items, from groceries to coal, could be obtained from this building and the new post office. The small shed on the left remained until the early 1970s; on the door during the Second World War were fixed the fire-watch duty rosters.

BARRACK COTTAGES IN AROUND 1906. These cottages were used as a barracks during the Napoleonic wars. Whether the building dates from that period or if it is earlier is not known. The extreme right end of the building was the officers' quarters. Beside the fireplace was an arch which led into the mess; this and the cooking area took up the remainder of the ground floor. The first floor was the dormitory, the internal walls being made of very large timbers and covered with lath and plaster. During the early sixties the building was entirely rebuilt, only the four outer walls remaining, and it is now one dwelling.

ANOTHER VIEW OF BARRACK COTTAGES, from the green in around 1906. It looks to be a hot high summer's day.

BISHOPSTONE CHURCH AND VILLAGE GREEN

BISHOPSTONE VILLAGE GREEN has two curious names, the Egg and the Hagg. The first name is still used, the second is recorded on the Pelham estate map of 1779. It is now registered as a village green. Also on the green are the almshouses built in memory of Mary Anne Catt. The first stone was laid by her nephew Thomas Cooper of Norton on 18 May 1857.

BARRACK COTTAGES AND THE COTTAGE. This postcard was photographed from the green during the early twenties.

BISHOPSTONE HOUSE in around 1952. During the 1930s this was the home of Denis Mackail, the author of many children's stories.

WHITE ROW COTTAGES, Nos 126 to 129, in around 1905. During the Second World War, the village air-raid shelter was dug into the bank opposite these cottages. It was made of railway sleepers and had a thatched roof to resemble a haystack, and was big enough to hold whist drives in. On VE night it was burned to the ground, by persons unknown.

THE VILLAGE FROM GRATTON FIELD. Most of the lovely elm trees remained until the onset of Dutch elm disease.

FIELD COTTAGES, Nos 137 and 138. This is a most charming view, taken by F.M. Pople in 1936. These cottages are some of the oldest in the village and were originally thatched. All farm cottages on the Earl of Chichester's estate were numbered consecutively starting at Stanmer Park, Bishopstone and Norton being 121 to 144. They then proceed to Foxhole Farm, Chyngton Farm and so on.

THE COTTAGE in around 1918. This house was built in 1906 by Mr Harry Willett, in the corner of Plummers Field. Over the years the farm has moved from one end of the village to the other, and this is now technically Manor Farm House.

THE ROAD JUST ABOVE BARRACK COTTAGES, constructed of flints and rammed chalk. The material was dug out from numerous chalkpits in the area. One such pit in Silver Lane was latterly used as the village rubbish tip.

AN EARLY VIEW OF THE VILLAGE, little altered today except for the metalled road and the wealth of elm trees around the church. Beyond the man sitting on the wall is the cattleyard and stackyard. These two areas were originally the Glebeland, and here stood the Glebe Barn.

THE VILLAGE IN EARLY SUMMER, dated 1913. New Cottages and Manor Farm buildings now stand on the left.

LOOKING TOWARDS NORTON AND THE DOWNS. During April 1954 much repair work was done to the church tower. While the scaffolding was up, Mr George Laughlin, the churchwarden, took this photograph.

NEW COTTAGES in around 1937, with one of Lionel Willett's steam engines standing in its usual place. Jim Westwood, Scamp and Lucy are walking up the road.

HARVEST TIME. In the foreground is one of the thatched hovels, and another steam engine can just be seen to the left.

THE HAMLET OF NORTON, photographed from the hill known as the Cricket Bat, in about 1905. Behind is the Norton Farm half of Beacon Hill. This hill is recorded as early as 1374 as *la Bekne*, and must have had signal fires built at the summit.

NORTON FROM THE CRICKET BAT in 1928. Lower Barn can be seen, and was the last thatched building in Norton. On the corner of the road is the garage with flat above. This housed the engine and battery rooms which produced the electricity for Little Hallands until 1935.

NORTON FARM HOUSE. Near the open windows are members of the Cooper family, who farmed here over a period of 150 years.

NORTON FARM COTTAGES. Nos 141 and 142. They must have been built for someone quite important; they are constructed of flint and dressed stone and bear the date 1597 over the door.

LITTLE HALLANDS. This is the largest house in Bishopstone or Norton and was probably named after the Pelham mansion at Halland. The lower portion is the oldest part of the house and the fine windows date from the eighteenth century. This photograph was taken during the ownership of F.D. Pirie Esquire. The house was used by him as a country home, together with Sir Adrian Pollock 'City Chamberlain of London' and the Hon. Lady Pollock and their daughters Anne (who married Cyril Asquith, later Lord Asquith of Bishopstone) and Betty McConnel (the actress and mimic Elizabeth Pollock).

LITTLE HALLANDS in around 1938, from the bedroom window of Rose Cottage. In the foreground is the tennis court, and the walnut tree is on the front lawn. In 1961 the property was sold and divided into three separate houses, some of which have been sub-divided again.

THE PUMPING STATION in around 1928. It was the home of the Laughlin family for sixty-seven years. The house stands on the parish boundaries of Bishopstone and Denton.

AT THE END OF THE ROAD, the pumping station built by the Newhaven and Seaford Water Company in 1899. The engines were coal-fired, the coal being delivered by horse and cart and later by steam traction engine. This photograph of 1920 also shows Poverty Farm, of which nothing exists today.

SECTION TWO

People and
Social Events

BISHOPSTONE SCHOOL in 1894, beside the front door of the schoolhouse. These children would have come from the village, and from Norton, Foxhole and Tidemills.

THE PLAYERS of a Little Hallands versus Norton Farm cricket match taking a break for tea in around 1928. These matches were held in the field behind Little Hallands on a specially-mown pitch; a marquee, ice-cream and teas were provided. Back row, left to right: -?-, -?-, Percy Laughlin, Maud Donald, Luke Asquith, -?-, Fred Collinson, Alexander Park, -?-.

MEMBERS OF THE FORD FAMILY outside the door of 143 Norton Farm.

A CHARMING GROUP OF YOUNG LADIES out for an afternoon walk. They pose for the photographer at the foot of the Shepherds' Steps. These ancient steps led to the top of Rookery Hill. In the background is the First Plantation.

THE FORD FAMILY in the garden of 137 Field Cottages in 1926. Back row, left to right: Arthur Ford, Connie Ford, Oliver Ford, Arthur Ford, Hugh Ford, Eric Ford, Bill Oliver, Maggie Ford, Tom Ford. Front row, left to right: Nancy Ford, Gladys Ford, Tom Ford, Norah Ford, Jean Ford, Kate Oliver, Fanny Ford, Jeannie Ford.

TOM FORD of 137 Field Cottages. Born in 1843, he worked for Mr Cooper of Norton as a shepherd, and was married on 5 December 1868 at Bishopstone to Mary Jane Coleman. They had ten children, five boys and five girls.

MARY FORD in the doorway of 137 Field Cottages.

EACH YEAR A TEA PARTY was given at the Manor House for the schoolchildren. This photograph was taken in 1929. Among the children seen here are Rob Burcham, Harold Grantham, Margaret Geering, Francis Gutsell, Cissy Cox, Don Moore, Dolly Geering, Rose Geering and David Larkin.

BOYS ENJOYING THEMSELVES AT THE PRODUCE SHOW of 1936, held on the Egg. As the village lads got older, they could augment their pocket money by shooting rats in the various barns around the farm, and would be paid so much per tail.

BISHOPSTONE WOMEN'S INSTITUTE FETE in the Manor House garden, June 1936. Back row, left to right: -?-, Miss Ridge, Miss Ridge, Maud Westwood, Evelyn Green, Maud Laughlin, Mrs Tuppen, Mrs F.M. Pople, Miss Warner, the Revd Squirrel, Mrs Squirrel, Mrs J. Meads, Miss Carpenter, -?-, Mrs Cross, Rachel Cross, Mrs G.A. Laughlin. Front row, left to right: Mrs Louisa Tattersall, Nigel Tuckley, -?-, Win Jenner, Miss Nancy Laughlin, Gladys Laughlin and children of the Manor School.

AT THE PRODUCE SHOW of 1938 held on the Egg. Back row, left to right: Derek Baker, -?-, -?-, -?-, Monica Moore, -?-, Toni Laughlin, Eileen West, Winnie Cox, Kathie Pilbeam, Christine Pople, Mrs Lishman, Maud Fowler, Miss Dawson, Mr Isted. Front row, left to right: Joyce Standen, -?-, Doreen Standen, Iris Cox, Margaret Cox.

ANOTHER HAPPY GROUP AT THE PRODUCE SHOW of 1938, partaking of tea and cakes. Among those seen here are Mr Isted, Nancy Laughlin, Maisie Green, Mona Miles and Win Jenner.

A STEADY HAND was needed for this game at the Produce Show. Left to right: -?-, -?-, Fred Collinson, -?-, -?-, -?-, Jack Meads, Percy Laughlin, -?-, Mrs Tattersall, -?-, -?-, Jack Young.

THE HON. LADY POLLOCK AND THE REVD SQUIRREL opening the church fête in the vicarage garden, 1937. Back row, left to right: Mrs Town, Mrs Cross, Mrs Burcham, Miss Nancy Laughlin, Miss Warner, -?-.

MOST OF THE CHILDREN FROM THE VILLAGE in *A Midsummer Night's Dream* at the church fête, 1937. Back row, left to right: -?-, Winnie Cox, Winnie Moore, Ethel Moore, Monica Moore, Toni Laughlin, Eileen West, Doreen Standen, Christine Pople. Middle row, left to right: Joyce Standen, -?-, Iris Cox, Gladys Laughlin, Jessie West, Jean Moore. Front row, left to right: Percy Cox, Denny Moore, -?-, -?-, Roger Smith, Stephen Moore, Alan Smith, -?-.

NIGEL TUCKLEY'S BIRTHDAY PARTY in the schoolhouse garden, 1935. Back row, left to right: Mrs Tuckley (headmistress), Miss Blann (teacher), Maud Westwood, Mrs G. Laughlin. Front row, left to right: Doreen Standen, Joyce Standen, Nigel Tuckley, Gladys Laughlin, Christine Pople, Mrs F.M. Pople.

SOME OF THE STAFF FROM LITTLE HALLANDS sitting on the Egg, Jubilee Day, 1935.

MR CHARLIE TUPPEN at the 1935 Produce Show. He still lives in the village, and has been here longer than anyone else. His father Tom Tuppen and his grandfather Alf Tuppen both lived and worked all their lives in the village.

THE ANNUAL PRODUCE SHOW was the village's largest social event. It was started in 1919 and continued until 1939. Numerous challenge cups and prizes were presented for all of the seventy classes. On the right stand Mr T. Standen and Mr J. Westwood.

ANOTHER GENERAL VIEW of the 1935 Produce Show.

MR JACK YOUNG in around 1936, verger at Bishopstone for many years. He was tragically killed riding his bicycle between Bishopstone and Newhaven.

THIS PHOTOGRAPH OF MR F.M. POPLE, farm secretary to Mr Lionel Willett, was taken in 1940. He was the air-raid warden and food control officer for Bishopstone. It was in his out-houses that the emergency supplies (in case of invasion) were stored.

WHIST DRIVE AND SOCIAL at the Village Hall, around 1947. Back row, left to right: Dewi James, Les Davis, Jack Jenner, Nick Parks, -?-, Rose Parks, Eileen Saunders, Mrs Jenner, -?-, -?-, Harry Cox, -?-, Mrs Jones, the Revd Jones, Colin Pople, Fred Laughlin, Percy Cox. Middle row: Dilys Brooks, Frank Pople, Mrs Tuppen, Iris Cox, Mrs Cox, Kit Goldsmith, Winnie Pople, -?-, Christine Pople, Fred Mitchell, Jean Moore, Joyce Standen, Gladys Laughlin. Front row: George Laughlin, Nancy Laughlin, Mrs Purbrook, John O'Gara.

THE INDUCTION OF THE REVD JONES outside the almshouses, 1946, with visiting clergy and Captain F. Stammers and Mr Percy Laughlin, the churchwardens.

BISHOPSTONE WOMEN'S INSTITUTE in 1948, portraying James Hurdis and three of his sisters. Left to right: Nancy Laughlin, Norah Price, Mrs Honeywood and Molly Simpson.

MEMBERS OF THE WOMEN'S INSTITUTE, 1955. Mrs Birch, Mrs Vaughan, Mrs W. Hunt, Mrs M. Laughlin, Mrs M.A. Simpson. By this time, members were no longer divided into 'ladies' and 'women', as was the case in 1920 when the Institute first met in the drawing room at Little Hallands.

MEMBERS OF THE WOMEN'S INSTITUTE in around 1956. Left to right: Mrs Cox, Mrs O'Malley, Mrs M. Laughlin, Mrs J. Willett, Mrs W. Hunt, Mrs F.M. Pople.

EACH CHRISTMAS THE CHURCH CHOIR went out carol-singing. One evening they would do Bishopstone Road, Station Road and Marine Drive, the second night the village and Norton. They are seen here outside White Row Cottages in around 1950.

FOR SEVERAL YEARS Bishopstone had its own football team. Members are shown here in around 1949, attending to the pitch. Back row, left to right: Gerald Woolmer, -?-, Vic Harris, Bob Moore, Jack Saunders, -?-, Vic Hampton, Johnny Gutsell. Front row, left to right: Trayton Standen, Sid Lambert, Smokey Everest, Wally Pannel.

MEMBERS OF THE FOOTBALL TEAM in around 1950. Back row, left to right: Billy Beard (father), Peter Hayward, -?-, Don Moore, Jim Morgan, Roy Tucknott, Alfred Hall, Vic Hampton, Harry Cox. Front row, left to right: Smokey Everest, Jack Saunders, Bob Moore, Percy Cox, Billy Beard (son), Denny Moore, Charlie Woolmer, Wally Pannel.

THE WEDDING OF TWO BISHOPSTONE RESIDENTS, Mr Bartlett and Mrs Jenner, on 14 October 1950. This photograph was taken beside the almshouses, where they made their home.

RESTORATION WORK TO THE INTERIOR of the village hall, during the winter of 1961. Here Mr G. Laughlin, Mr W. Baden and Mr P. Laughlin are seen putting up the new ceiling. This building was originally the school, given by the Earl of Chichester in 1849. In 1883 it was enlarged and, by 1895, Kelly's Directory stated that there was provision for eighty children.

A REGULAR EVENT EACH WINTER was the meet of the Southdown Hunt. They are seen here in the early 1950s, passing New Cottages.

MR TRAYTON STANDEN ON 'SUGAR', returning past Bishopstone House after a day's hunting.

ANOTHER MEET OF THE SOUTHDOWN HUNT, some time in the mid-1950s. They are gathered beside the village hall.

THE HUNT MOVING OFF on a grey winter's morning. The Green appears very devoid of trees, compared with today.

MR BOB ROOK AND MRS WIN JENNER watch the Hunt go past Barrack Cottages in around 1957.

MR FRED COLLINSON riding with the hunt outside Little Hallands during the 1930s.

SECTION THREE

Farming

A TEAM OF FOUR SUSSEX DRAUGHT OXEN belonging to Mr Harry Willett, photographed in Watland Furlong. Each pair is coupled by a wooden yoke; they are pulling a Sussex wagon.

MR STACE PLOUGHING WAY FIELD in 1896, with a team of six oxen. Bishopstone Road can just be seen in the distance.

THATCHED RICKS standing at the bottom of Beacon Hill. Just visible beside the furthest ricks are several small thatched flax ricks. Flax was grown at Bishopstone for many years, mainly in these fields and in Way Field. There were also trial plots grown for the Government of Northern Ireland.

A WINTRY VIEW TOWARDS MANOR FARM HOUSE in around 1938. Although covered by snow, several interesting farming features can be seen, including the shepherd's caravan and a Sussex wagon.

STEAM PLOUGHING ENGINES belonging to Mr Lionel Willett stand outside New Cottages.

HARVESTING was made a lot easier at Norton Farm following the purchase of their first combine, seen here during the mid-1950s.

PLOUGHING IN HAM LANE, NORTON FARM, during the 1940s. All the fields in the parish have names; several of those used today appear on the Pelham estate map of 1777. Ham Lane consisted then of 52 acres, 1 rod and 27 perches.

HERE IS A NEW IDEA of crawler design, efficiency and economy in farm haulage. It is an International tractor (TD6) model, supplied by Messrs Harper & Eede, agricultural engineers of Lewes, at work on Mr F. Collinson's farm at Bishopstone. The engine is a diesel and runs on crude oil.

'POLLARD', A SHEPHERD AT NORTON FARM, with his trusted dogs. In his poem, *The Favourite Village*, James Hurdis refers to the practice of shepherds trapping wheatears which were eaten as a delicacy in Brighton. When Hurdis found a bird so caught he would release it and leave a few pence in its place.

THE STEAM PLOUGHING ENGINES were sold for scrap and cut up on site during the 1950s, a decision regretted by all ever since.

A RARE PHOTOGRAPH OF THE FORGE in Silver Lane. Nothing is now left of this building except for a few walls. The flat metal disc on the ground to the right of the door can still be seen there today.

CATTLE IN WHITEGATE FIELD having an early morning feed during the winter of 1960.

A TRANQUIL AND BEAUTIFULLY-FRAMED VIEW of the village from the rookery, on a spring afternoon in around 1954.

SECTION FOUR

Little Hallands

A VERY INTERESTING PHOTOGRAPH OF LITTLE HALLANDS taken in around 1905. It shows the front door and most of the windows in their original positions. Some time after 1907 the house was remodelled, the front door moved to the left and most of the windows resited. This house was the home of James Hurdis (1710–1769), who was collector of customs at Newhaven and brother of Thomas Hurdis, private secretary to the Duke of Newcastle. It was also the home of his son James Hurdis DD (1763–1801), the poet and vicar of Bishopstone.

JAMES HURDIS aged 29, painted by T. Sprink of Chelsea from a 1792 miniature by Teed. From 1689 till 1844 the benefice was under sequestration. James Hurdis was the only exception, being appointed vicar by Bishop Ashburnham, prompted by Lord Pelham, in October 1791. The living was then increased by a payment from Queen Anne's Bounty, yielding a net income of £45 per annum.

DURING THE TIME OF DR RUTHERFORD a series of photographs of Little Hallands was taken by W.R. Wynter of Broad Street, Seaford. This one, looking west, shows a herbaceous border, part of the front lawn and the walnut tree.

THE DINING ROOM AT LITTLE HALLANDS photographed some time before 1907. This is the only room that can be positively identified today. These and the following three photographs became known after mention in a letter to *Country Life*, 8 October 1981.

THIS IS THOUGHT TO BE the front hall at Little Hallands. On the left is a splendid eighteenth-century continental chest. This room, as with all others on the ground floor of the house, was remodelled after 1907, and then formed part of the smoking room.

THE DRAWING ROOM, very well furnished with period pieces. Most of the fabrics have an Arts and Crafts appearance to them, so typical of a country house during the early years of this century. This room originally had a fireplace at either end, but the one shown has disappeared.

THIS WAS DR RUTHERFORD'S LIBRARY at Little Hallands, alas, another room that was later remodelled when it became the front hall. William Gunion Rutherford was born in Glasgow in 1853. A classical scholar, he was educated at Glasgow High Scool, thence to St Andrew's University and Balliol. He was elected Headmaster of Westminster School in 1883 and remained there until he retired in 1901. He was profoundly dissatisfied with the revised version of the New Testament and in 1900 brought out a new translation of the Epistle to the Thessalonians and to the Corinthians. One can imagine this great scholar working at the mahogany secretaire desk, surrounded by his books. He died here in 1907 and is buried in the churchyard at Bishopstone.

ELSIE AND DORIS, two of the maids from Little Hallands, in 1930. Exactly what they are doing in the yard with the piglets is anybody's guess.

MR ALEXANDER PARK AND MR JACK MEADS, both in turn head gardeners at Little Hallands, in around 1936. They had a staff of at least five or six in the garden, producing most types of fruit, vegetables, cut flowers and so on, for a large household both here and in London.

MR PERCY LAUGHLIN in 1930 working on the tennis court at Little Hallands with the Atco motor mower. The machine was used here for thirty-eight years.

MR ALEXANDER PARK, HEAD GARDENER, standing outside Little Hallands. He retired in 1933 after thirty-six years' service to the family of F.D. Pirie.

A BUMPER CROP OF POTATOES in the kitchen garden of Little Hallands in August 1945. Resting on their forks and taking a well-deserved break are Mr Percy Cox and Mr Jack Young. The kitchen garden is now Bishopstone Nurseries.

THE NEXT FIVE PHOTOGRAPHS show some of the cars that belonged to F.D. Pirie Esquire of Little Hallands. This is the 50 hp Rolls Royce, taken in 1923.

THE CHAUFFEUR Mr George Laughlin sits in the 1923 11.9 hp grey Morris Cowley tourer.

THIS SPLENDID CAR was bought in March 1928 and is a 15.9 hp red Morris Overseas tourer YF 884.

ALL THE CARS were kept in immaculate condition as can be seen here. This 16 hp red Morris saloon was bought in April 1929.

ANOTHER CAR IN PRISTINE CONDITION is this 21 hp black Wolseley saloon, bought on 5 March 1933. All these vehicles were in constant use, going to and from London and to many social events and race meetings throughout the country.

SECTION FIVE

Snow

THE WINTER of 1938 saw an exceedingly heavy fall of snow which blocked the road. Beside the gate can be seen one of the steam engines.

AS A RESULT of the 1938 snow, Norton was completely cut off. A path was dug out by hand along the entire length of the road. This shows the last section of snow being removed outside Bishopstone House. Left to right: Gladys Laughlin, Rob Meads, Jack Meads, Les Weller, Percy Laughlin.

ANOTHER VIEW OF THE SNOW during 1938. The only other time in living memory that there was as much snow as this was during the winter of 1962/3.

THE ROOKERY OR DUKE'S RIDE in around 1954. In those days the flint wall was intact. Most of the beech trees are still there today, but alas, the wonderful elm trees have gone, due to Dutch elm disease. So we leave Bishopstone and walk off in the direction of Seaford.

SEAFORD

After Bishopstone's timeless tranquillity, the bustle of modern Seaford might lead the visitor to conclude that there is no history here, but it is all around us. On the grassy western slope of Seaford Head is a U-shaped ridge with its mouth at the cliff edge: two thousand years ago this was an earth rampart thrown up as a primitive defence by our Iron Age ancestors. Worked flints from those same times, if not earlier, surface periodically. In 1987 for example, excavations for the laying of a new gas main in High Street revealed a cache of fifteen Stone Age axeheads. In Victorian times, an archaeological dig to the north of the Iron Age rampart uncovered Roman funeral urns and, more recently, skeletons found on the beach after major cliff falls show how far their burial ground extended.

When the Normans came to Seaford after the 1066 invasion, they found a settlement beside a natural, undeveloped harbour. This had been formed where the River Ouse made its way into the sea, after flowing more than two miles parallel with the shore behind a vast shingle bank. Before long, Seaford was a busy port exporting Sussex wool and importing the wines, silks, spices and other continental luxuries the Normans had been missing.

They built a church, up on the skyline where it would be a landmark for sailors. Through 900 years' fire and pestilence, the ravages of weather and cross-channel raiders, part of that original church remains. The arched base of the tower, exposed on the south but within the vestry on the north, was part of the nave built around 1090.

Another very solid reminder of those prosperous times can be seen today in the southern corner of Church Street car park. Known locally as 'the crypt', it has been identified by experts as 'the undercroft of a medieval merchant's house.' Records show that at one time fifty-eight different wool exporters used Seaford, three-quarters of the goods left in Seaford ships, and seventeen of the exporters were in fact Seaford merchants. Such a vital seaport was soon drawn into the Cinque Ports system; the earliest record of our membership yet discovered is dated 1229.

A number of towns along the Kent and Sussex coast were pledged to send ships, men and stores when called on by the sovereign in time of war. In return, they were granted privileges in such matters as claiming tolls and duties, salvage from shipwrecks, trying and sentencing prisoners, and parliamentary election. From 1298 to 1832 (with a 200-year break) Seaford was represented by two Members of Parliament. From Tudor times, the administrative centre of the town was the old town hall in South Street, still with us today, as is a stone arch removed from the dungeon and now set into the wall of the Crouch Gardens in East Street.

By the sixteenth century, the same drift of shingle which had formed Seaford harbour was destroying it. The passage to the sea silted up so that ships could not enter and the river began to break through the shingle bank at points further west. In 1545, for example, there was some opening near today's Sailing Club premises. We know a battle was fought there, when a French fleet (two days after causing the *Mary Rose* to capsize at Southsea) tried to land but was driven off, with the loss of one hundred lives, by Sir Nicholas Pelham and his followers. That area has since been called after the Pelham family crest . . . The Buckle.

Though Henry VIII granted the town its first charter and Queen Elizabeth I presented a little silver mace (now on display at The Downs), nothing could be done to retrieve the situation and for nearly a century the townsfolk tried to live off the sea, from fishing and shipwrecks (recalling the Cinque Ports privilege). They earned an evil reputation for their treatment of drowning sailors whose ships were lured ashore by false navigation lights. A good deal of smuggling also went on.

The population dwindled so much and there was so little left to steal that by 1539 it was not thought worthwhile to defend the place, and all cannon were dismantled. After a variety of sitings, one Tudor piece eventually found its way to the corner of Steyne Road and Crouch Lane, where it remains to this day. It no longer protects the flint wall from damage by the hubs of passing cartwheels, but reminds us of those far-off heady times.

Though Seaford kept a low profile in the sixteenth and seventeenth centuries, there was some religious persecution, and so we have Captain John Seaman emulating the Pilgrim Fathers by sailing to the New World, purchasing land from the native Indians, and founding Seaford, Long Island, New York State.

A political revival after the Civil War prompted Seaford to claim its parliamentary double representative again, and for many years 'the 'lections' were a considerable source of income, with meetings, balls, dinners, parades . . . and bribes, bringing a kind of prosperity to the sadly depressed little town. Seaford was one of the 'rotten boroughs', in the political pocket of 'the greatest election-monger', the Duke of Newcastle.

In 1761 the Duke introduced a bill to Parliament allowing a mill to be built across the tidal creek near the shore opposite Bishopstone – all that remained of the old river – and Tidemills village came into being. Barges arrived with grain and departed with flour; eventually, sixteen pairs of millwheels were working eighteen hours a day, the mill supplying the whole county and sixty men being employed, most of whom lived with their families in the village.

It was here in 1795 that the mutineers of the Oxfordshire Militia stole the *Lucy* laden with flour. The fate of Tidemills is a story in itself; a few flint walls remain today to remind us.

The Martello Tower was built in around 1809 near Seaford Head, for the same reason that militia had been brought into the area: it was feared that the French would invade. They never did, and the tower went through periods of neglect till Mr Tom Funnell turned it into an entertainment centre. Some seventy years after his successful occupation, the tower is again a hive of activity and a tourist attraction, as Seaford Museum.

When the Reform Act of 1832 swept away redundant parliamentary rights such as Seaford's, the town entered yet another period of decline. This was short-lived because the craze for seaside resorts had begun. The London Brighton and South Coast Railway extended their line to Seaford in 1864, and optimism grew that the town would prosper again as visitors arrived to create a 'second Brighton'. Developers moved in with grand plans for rows of boarding houses; they laid out their roads, began building . . . and left. For almost a hundred years terraces like Pelham Place and West View stood in splendid isolation as reminders of yet another sterile phase in the town's history.

'The sea will have its own' – and there are accounts from as early as the fourteenth century of the town being inundated when breaches occurred at weak spots in the shingle bank. The 1875 flooding may not have been the worst ever, but newspaper reports and photographs ensured it was widely publicized. The Common (old river bed) was covered and West House, Marine Terrace and other buildings in Steyne Road (*le Quayside*) were damaged. Six years later the first serious attempt to protect Seaford with a sea-wall began.

The First World War brought thousands of troops, on their way to France or in training. They called Sutton Place, used as an army signal school, 'the Khaki College'. Fine air and green fields near the sea brought convalescent homes and boarding schools to the district; what is believed to be the first such home in the country opened in 1859 at 'Talland', Lower High Street. A few of the schools remain today, while others changed their use, and still more have been demolished to make way for houses.

On a walk through the town centre one can readily pick out interesting buildings that have witnessed history; the former York House is an example, with its knapped flint façade, or the three-storey building in Lower High Street dressed with mathematical tiles. I hope this introduction has disproved a newcomer's observation that 'nothing happened here between the river changing its course and Safeway's opening', and that readers will enjoy the following pages as much as I have enjoyed preparing them.

Many photographs are from the huge Museum collection, and I warmly acknowledge the help of George Jakens, Denis Rogers and other members. Kind folk, lifelong Seaforders, have taken time and trouble to answer my questions, as well as agreeing to appear in the book. I have tried to contact everybody on this point, and apologize if any have been missed. Photographic sources have been checked as far as possible; if any acknowledgements have been overlooked, apologies are tendered.

SECTION SIX

Coastline

Coastguard Station, Cuckmere Haven, Seaford

COASTGUARD STATION overlooking Cuckmere Haven, 1912. It was vital to guard the haven in readiness for smugglers and shipwrecks. Small boats could make an easy landing with contraband, or sail upriver to Alfriston. Larger vessels which ran aground here included the Danish Schooner *Mogens Koch* in December 1929. The ten-man crew was rescued in 85 m.p.h. gusts of wind and torrential rain by Newhaven lifeboat. Coastguards operated here from 1806 to 1972.

CUCKMERE HAVEN from west slope of Haven Brow. Some Sherlock Holmes devotees say that this area was Sir Arthur Conan Doyle's inspiration for 'Fulworth' in one of the last stories, *The Adventure of the Lion's Mane*. It would be agreeable to think that the two gentlemen here surveying the tranquil scene were the great detective and his loyal Doctor Watson reincarnated.

Rough Seas, Seaford Cliffs.

THE CLIFFS. This postcard in the Mercread series was written from 'Eversley' on the seafront on 24 September 1913. (Mercread is believed to be a corruption of Mercredesburn, the ancient name for Seaford – 'the town on the riverbank'.) One wonders how many tons of chalk have fallen during the intervening years; certainly the naked eye can appreciate what inroads have been made by Seaford's fierce tides.

SEAFRONT WORK. During his time (1893–1928) as consultant surveyor to Seaford Local Board (later Urban District Council) Mr Boyd Archibald Miller (above on the left) saw many advances in sea defence, drainage and other public works. In 1900, there were fifty-eight groynes between Cliff End and Tidemills. Below, the sewer outfall pipe when laid under the seafront in 1910.

THE BEACH LOOKING WEST, 1890. Those wishing to bathe changed into their neck-to-ankle costumes in the bathing machines, which were then rolled to the water's edge. Down steps, the bathers thus entered the sea while preserving their modesty. The aproned woman here follows the age-old seaside tradition of spreading washing (or damp clothing) on the beach to dry. Tents later replaced bathing machines.

THE PROMENADE TOWARDS NEWHAVEN. Some fifty years later, the biggest change in the scene is the number of groynes dividing the shingle beach. Still people sit on the beach or bathe in the sea, still shelter is needed and a longshoreman is in attendance. Note the invalid chair with driving levers, just visible behind the man standing at the promenade edge.

Streets

CLINTON PLACE LOOKING WEST, 1930. This terrace was built when the London Brighton and South Coast Railway extended the line to Seaford (1864). Originally No. 1 on the corner of Church Road was the only shop; the others were converted later, and No. 3 once housed the Urban District Council offices. The street was first called Terminus Road, going no further than the railway station. Unusually, the trees grew not on the pavement but in the road.

CHURCH STREET in around 1906. Someone spotted the photographer setting up his tripod and camera, and folk in their Sunday best turned out to be recorded for future generations. Most of the cottages on the left were bombed during the Second World War, but the beautiful tree on the right was lost much earlier. It died when damaged by trench-digging for roadworks.

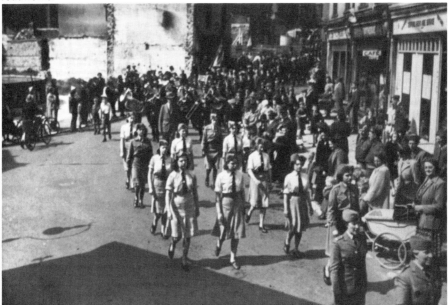

CHURCH STREET at junction of South Street, 1941/2. Members of Seaford's Women's Junior Air Corps (female counterpart of the Air Cadet Corps), led by Mrs Marsh, take part in a parade of units including the Fire Service and British Legion (with band). The space occupied by an emergency water tank and the damaged walls beyond show where the bomb fell.

SOUTH STREET looking towards Seaford Head, 1906. The site of the second shop from the left is now the forecourt of The High shopping mall. The garden in which the tree stood became the setting for the first Baptist church, later converted into shops. The lady in the pale flowing gown stands at the mouth of High Street.

THE STEYNE, 1906. It is not hard to imagine this road in medieval times, when known as le Quayside, fronting a shallow harbour whose waters covered the land in the foreground. The Jubilee drinking fountain originally stood in the road further east outside the New Inn (now the Wellington) but it proved to be a traffic hazard. These days, it can be found in the Salts Recreation Ground.

LOWER HIGH STREET looking north-east, 1929. Little except the pace of life has altered in sixty years in this quiet corner of the old town, helped by the introduction of a modern one-way traffic system. In April 1795 it was the setting for frightful scenes as the Oxfordshire Militia mutineers rampaged through with fixed bayonets, seeking vengeance on the butchers and bakers who had cheated them.

BROAD STREET in about 1930. The post office, extreme left, was moved to Church Street in 1977, and shops now stand on this site. Replacements for these trees were planted to commemorate the 1953 coronation, marked by a plaque on the post office wall. By 1960, the roots were again pushing up the pavements; the road is sadly leafless today.

SECTION EIGHT

Shops and Businesses

WOOD'S STORES, 19–23 High Street, with Mr Dennis's car. Described in a 1900 directory as a general store and drapers, nine years later the stores' advertisement featured 'Harris Wiltshire Bacon a speciality' and 'House and Estate Agency'. The shop-fronts may have been modernized since, but the first floor façade has hardly altered.

SALE AT ASHBY & CO, 19 Clinton Place (Terminus Road), photographed by W.R. Wynter of Broad Street. To this day, these premises continue as a ladies' outfitters. It is interesting that only one member of the waiting crowd is bareheaded. Was this to save time in trying on the bargain hats, once she was inside?

W. GREEN, BUTCHER, 38 High Street. A number of ancient cottages formerly stood on this site on the south side of High Street. Some of them were built of flint, or had small diamond-pane windows. All were swept away during redevelopment in 1894. Among those people photographed here are George Morley, Tom Tourell and Jack Marshall.

E.G. LEA, BAKER AND CONFECTIONER, BROAD STREET, 1890. An advertisement of around this date described the business as 'Miller, corn merchant, baker and confectioner. Garden and flower seeds and all requisites for garden purposes'. The premises, on the south corner of Sutton Road, remain much the same today, the only alterations being to some windows; the plaque over the side door, inscribed 'EGL 1885' is still there.

W. HOWELL, GROCER, 57 HIGH STREET. During the Second World War, bombs fell on this part of the town; buildings from Howell's corner as far as the Cinque Ports public house (formerly the Rising Sun) and round into East Street were demolished. One of the first peacetime projects was to erect council flats on the site. The leaping chimney from the pub to No. 47 survived, and was only removed in recent years.

SEAFORD MOTOR WORKS AND GARAGE, STEYNE ROAD, corner of Ashurst Road, 1912. The proprietor Ben French had other premises in Newhaven. In 1910 he bought a secondhand 20 hp Humber car for £160; it may well be one of those shown here. The building still houses a car showroom; it and the neighbouring house are easily recognizable.

BLATCHINGTON ROAD: MISS QUEENIE MORLING'S RETIREMENT, 1954. Morling's building firm was founded in 1844 by Miss Morling's grandfather. She was first a clerk, then secretary, for forty-nine and a half years and received her retirement gifts from the oldest employee Mr E. Banks (third from left, front row). Although horse-drawn carts had earlier transported materials to sites, by 1954 the presence of 'Captain' the twelve-year-old shire gelding, was purely traditional.

B. BERRY AND SONS, AGRICULTURAL ENGINEERS, Crouch Lane. The forge was purchased in 1928 from FitzGerald Charity by Gilbert Newton Berry, a registered farrier; his sons Arthur and John later joined the firm. Shoeing hacking and work-horses gradually ceased as tastes and vehicles changed, but farming implements continued to be made and repaired, and lawn mowers – 'motor, horse or hand' – were supplied and overhauled. Today the business is called Frank's Forge, specializing in wrought-ironwork, though still maintaining mowers. Standing left to right: Stephen Watts, Jonathon Carthew, Richard Seely. Seated: Frank Haynes, Dick Kneller.

SECTION NINE

Buildings

THE BAY APARTMENTS, PELHAM ROAD, 1870. Little changed in appearance or name today, this building replaced a charming balconied house, formerly the home of the Beane and Allfree families, which was demolished in around 1860. The cottages to the left met the same fate, succeeded by the Bay Hotel, now renamed the Lord Admiral.

THE SURREY CONVALESCENT HOME, at the western end of Seaford. When building was in progress in December 1888, the schooner *Mary Davis* was wrecked on the beach nearby. The contractor struck a bargain to buy part of the cargo of Portland stone for £20, and it was incorporated in the staircase and landing of the new home.

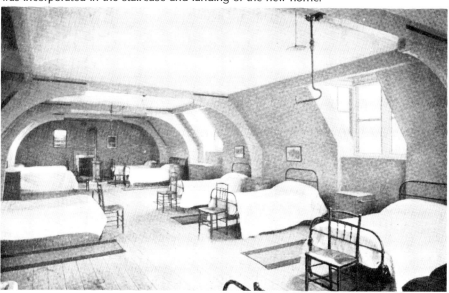

What to See in Seaford for Twopence.

THE MARTELLO TOWER

NO. 74,

Built about the year 1800 at a cost of £18,000 this Tower was purchased in 1911 by T. Funnell and is opened up more than any other one along the coast. In converting it into an Open Air Skating Rink and Tea Rooms (and proposed Sea Water Baths), it was necessary to cut three holes through walls seven feet thick.

The Moat is 360 feet round and contains 10,000 square feet of skating surface. A fine cement staircase and chimney piece has been constructed. The Magazine with its fourteen feet thick and the old fresh water tank can still be seen.

In the Tower is to be seen one of the most wonderful inlaid table tops in the world (made by T. Funnell, the proprietor), which occupied thirteen years (evenings) to construct, and which was awarded a bronze medal and diploma at the Crystal Palace 1911. Over 20,000 pieces of wood of ten varieties were used.

THE TOWER IS THE COOLEST PLACE IN SEAFORD FOR TEAS.

Pot of Tea, Roll and Butter - 5d.
To View the Tower Only - 2d.

HANDBILL FOR THE MARTELLO TOWER, presented by Mr Tom Funnell, proprietor. Its history before occupation by Mr Funnell was not so happy. Built as part of a chain of fortresses along the south-east coast to be a first line of defence against any cross-Channel invasion, it had been treated indifferently in peacetime. Its current use as Seaford Museum has brought it to life again.

CROUCHFIELD HOTEL. Originally the home of the Danby family, this old house took its name from the plot of land shown on the town tithe map adjacent to The Crouch (from *croix* or cross, after the paths that intersected there). An extension was built at the turn of the century, but in 1966 the whole building was demolished to make way for the new Constitutional Club.

ROSTREVOR, SUTTON PARK ROAD, 1925. The house stood on the corner of Stafford Road and was the home of Dr Charles C. Elliot. When it was demolished in around 1936, to make way for the large building now occupied by Caffyn's, a new house with the same name was erected on the seafront, near the site of Blatchington Battery.

ADVERTISEMENT FOR THE EMPIRE CINEMA. The cinema was built in Sutton Road by Mr Bravery in 1913; he already had a picture house in Brooklyn Road. Silent films were augmented by live performances: memories include a 'strong man' wielding barbells, a bugler playing an instrument sounded in the Afghan War some thirty years before, and *Scrooge*, adapted from Dickens's *Christmas Carol*, by local actors. In 1939 the Empire burned down and was never rebuilt.

THE POLICE STATION, CHICHESTER ROAD, 1939, sandbagged against enemy bomb damage. The local constabulary moved here in 1896 from a thatched cottage on the east corner of High Street and Crouch Lane. Since 1969 the station has been in purpose-built premises in Church Street. For 127 years the authority was entitled the East Sussex Police Force; on 1 January 1968 it became the Sussex Constabulary.

SEAFORD COUNCIL OFFICES, 1937, at the junction of East Street and Bramber Lane, with decorations for the Coronation of King George VI and Queen Elizabeth. Coldstream House now stands on the site. In the background are the lofty premises of the Seaside Convalescent Home, where Bramber Close and Steyne Close now stand. Nearer the camera is Martello Cottage, with us to this day.

THE GOLF HOUSE. Seaford Golf Club, the oldest in Sussex, opened in August 1887, one of its founders being a descendant of Jane Austen. The course was laid across the Downs above Seaford Head, and was 300 feet at its highest point. Accommodation was in a 'tin hut' adjoining the cottage of Reuben Russell, the shepherd, whose wife obliged by cooking chops brought by golfers for their lunch. In 1905 the club was re-titled Seaford Head Club, when the original name was taken to a new course at Blatchington.

DEMOLITION OF THE OLD TREE INN, 1965, on the corner of High Street and Broad Street. Possibly dating from Tudor times, the inn played an important part in the town's political heyday in the eighteenth century. Election dinners were held with many a speech and more than a few bribes, in the bad old 'rotten borough' days. A big piece of the town's history went with this demolition; modern shops now stand on the site.

UNDERCROFT OF MEDIEVAL MERCHANT'S HOUSE and superstructure, known locally as 'The Crypt' and 'The Folly'. For centuries this historic treasure was hidden behind Church Street and Pinders Square buildings. Enemy bomb damage during the Second World War led to their clearance, and the wooden Folly was removed later. The low flint building remains in the south corner of the police station car park, awaiting suitable attention.

SECTION TEN

People

PATRONS OF THE PELHAM ARMS, OFF HIGH STREET. Close inspection will reveal that only eight characters here are human. It is a pity that nothing remains today of the mural so vividly depicting our smuggling, wrecking ancestors. The pub was originally called the Duke of Cumberland's Head, and once had as its landlord Israel Medhurst, captain of the lifeboat and sometime coastguard, who lies buried in the shadow of the parish church.

THE TOWN BAND. Formed in 1922 with a loan of £20 from the British Legion to buy instruments (then including woodwind as well as brass), the band first rehearsed in an upstairs room at Woolgar's Forge in Place Lane. Above, photographed in 1924 in the garden of York House (now built over) on the corner of High Street and Saxon Lane, and with the Old Tree Inn in the background, the players include long-serving members of the Morling, Kennett, Lambert and Costick families. The vicar, Revd E.H. Phillips, stands far left. By the 1960s when the snapshot below was taken in the Crouch Gardens, they had become 'Seaford Silver Band', continuing to fulfil engagements near and far.

THE DUKE AND DUCHESS OF SPARTA (later King Constantine I and Queen Sophie of Greece) with their daughter, photographed on the beach near the Esplanade Hotel by the Princess Victoria, 1905. That same year, King Edward VII stayed at the hotel. Local excitement at his visit was greatly increased by his arrival in a motor car. Photograph reproduced by gracious permission of Her Majesty The Queen. Copyright reserved.

AFTERMATH OF THE GREAT STORM: MARINE TERRACE, STEYNE ROAD, 1875. After West House, this building was one of the worst affected. Its position facing up the Causeway was particularly vulnerable, and help was needed to clear up the damage. The *Sussex Advertiser* recorded that 'the first thing to do was to provide quarters for the poor creatures who had been rendered homeless ... and the sufferers were removed to houses in Pelham Place.'

MAJOR T. CROOK AND FOOTBALLERS. Major Crook helped launch a football team, playing on the common, in 1882. They were known as Seaford Rovers and won the Sussex Junior Cup in 1888 and 1910. Players here include John Major (fourth from left), who became team captain in 1886, and Bert Chambers (seated fifth from left).

With all good wishes
Nadia Sokoloff

NADIA SOKOLOFF, CONTRALTO WITH THE QUEER QUAKERS CONCERT PARTY, 1912. These enter-
tainers, so called because of their Puritan costumes, came every summer to amuse
residents and visitors alike. They were led by Edward and Lilly Pritchard (soprano), their
visits eagerly anticipated in an age with few outside distractions from the daily round.
Between the wars, Sir Ben Greet and his players continued the tradition of bringing live
entertainment to Seaford.

BAINBRIDGE HOUSE, 1923. Philanthropist Emerson Bainbridge brought the Swiss chalet from the Paris Exhibition of 1900 to a site off Steyne Road. Until its demolition over sixty years later (when Bainbridge Close was erected there) it served as a young people's holiday home and hostel. These girls were from St Jude's Church Club, West Ham. The toddler was the matron's child. The variety of hair styles and trimmings is a study in itself.

SEAFORD FIRE BRIGADE'S MERRYWEATHER APPLIANCE, with its ninety-five foot escape ladder, in front of their headquarters in Dane Road, 1939. Part of Safeway's store now covers the site. Back row, left to right: F. Gentry, J. Kent, D. Billings, A. Richardson. Front row, left to right: L. Squibb, A. Green, J. Reeves, G. Morling.

'JACK AND JILL': SEAFORD CHILDREN'S THEATRE, 1954, produced by Kathleen Marsh and presented at the Queen's Hall, Broad Street. In this photograph, kindly lent and identified by Graham Tubb, the players are: Back row, left to right: Geoffrey Beal, Raymond Beard, Colin Bell (dame), Ken Green, Pauline Bell, Elizabeth Green, Pam Forshaw, Lesley Bryant, David Hurst. Front row, left to right: Jack Beal, Julie Berry (fairy), Wendy Beal, Trixie Jane Bennett, Carolyne Flegg (Jill), Graham Tubb (Jack).

SEAFORD YOUNG MUSICIANS was founded in 1972 and, like Seaford Museum, had its headquarters at West House. Still going strong and with the same director, there are now 110 members of various ages playing a wide range of instruments. Back row, left to right: Sue Burnett, Margaret Lake, Alastair McCapra, Pat White (founder/director). Front row, left to right: Neil McCapra, Nicholas Lake, Katy Lewis, Fiona McCapra. Seated: Jackie Young.

FIRST AID PARTY, The Crouch. During the Second World War, men and women were trained in first aid as a vital part of home defences. Seaford's air-raids included several where homeward-bound enemy planes jettisoned surplus bombs. Back row, left to right: -?-. Bill Urry, Les Lambert. Front row, left to right: -?-, Jack Shinn, Frank Nail, Colin Cameron, George Laughlin. Note the car's stacked stretchers and white-edged mudguards and running-board.

ST JOHN AMBULANCE NURSES,The Crouch, summer 1942. An annexe planned for children was built at the Seaside Convalescent Home, but requisitioned as a first aid post, staffed by these nurses, at the outbreak of the Second World War. Included here are: Misses Randall, Grundy, Joan and Yseult King, Hillyard, Maisie Vine, Romer, Danby, Peggy Foster, Marjorie Brasher, Harding, Shelton, Eileen Simmons, LeStrange and Potts, and Mesdames Vine, Foster, Goodsell, Royle, Urry, Foyle, Libeau, Whittaker and Turrell.

SECTION ELEVEN

Churches

INTERIOR OF THE PARISH CHURCH OF ST LEONARD. This card, postmarked 1915, was sent from Edgland Terrace, Chichester Road, and includes the comment 'The town is full of the khaki boys.' Some interesting church features at this time, long since removed, are the altar decoration and the gracefully branched lamp standards. On the extreme right, the unique carving of the Bible scenes on the historied capital shows up sharply.

117

ST PETER'S CHURCH, BLATCHINGTON, INTERIOR. If 'Evelyn' – who sent this postcard to Gravesend in 1908 – visited the church today, she would see many changes. Major alterations took place in 1960 and 1966: pews, pulpit, organ, choir stalls and font were removed or re-sited to give additional seating space. The scripture quotations have disappeared, and the plain stone altar was installed in 1970. Registers date from 1563 and include entries about soldiers and their families from the nearby barracks.

ST LEONARD'S PARISH CHURCH OUTLINED IN GASLIGHT to mark the coronation of King George V and Queen Mary in 1911. Other celebrations were a procession of decorated vehicles (horse and cart, pony and trap) which included a May Queen ceremony, and a triumphal arch across Clinton Place, built and manned by the Fire Brigade.

SEAFORD LADIES' COLLEGE installed this window on the north of the parish church in the 1950s. It depicts (left to right) St Richard Bishop of Chichester, the Good Shepherd, and St Catherine. The dedication reads: 'To the glory of God and in memory of Seaford Ladies College whose members worshipped here 1900–1953.'

THE CATHOLIC CHURCH OF ST THOMAS MORE, INTERIOR. Catherine Giles's Stations of the Cross, painted in egg tempera on wood, are a special feature of the church. Opened in 1936, it was only the second Catholic church dedicated to St Thomas More. The first incumbent was Revd Father R.G. Webb, who conducted services at Annecy Convent until the congregation raised enough money to buy land and build the church.

THE BAPTIST CHURCH, BROAD STREET, 1971. From its first site on the north corner of High Street and South Street (which exists today, almost unidentifiable behind shopfronts), the church came here in around 1908. Sixty-five years later it moved again, to Belgrave Road, and the Broad Street building was replaced with shops.

SECTION TWELVE

Events

WEDDING OF WALTER WOOLGAR AND HARRIET GREEN. Thus, two ancient Seaford families were united; the earliest known record of a Woolgar is dated 1685. Some seventy years after Harriet wore it, her wedding dress was presented to Seaford Museum. Walter was a talented footballer, goalkeeper and captain of Seaford Rovers and a County player. During the First World War, the couple were licensees of the Old Tree Inn, where this photograph was taken.

GARDEN PARTY AT TELSEMAURE, ESPLANADE, 1900. The Crook family were staunch and generous supporters of Seaford Congregational church, and frequently opened the grounds of their home for Sunday School treats, fund-raising bazaars and the like. The first Seaford house to be gas-lit, it had been built in 1860 and was demolished in 1937. The name was formed from the initial letters of the family's first names.

PART OF TABLEAU IN TELSEMAURE MUSEUM: Burke and Willis at Coopers Creek, Australia. Reporting on a bazaar, the *East Sussex News* of 10 August 1888 said: 'An observatory was open at a trifling charge and a fine art gallery and museum were interesting. Specimens were exhibited of saltpetre, potash, a ship and a very effective lifesize representation of Burke, Willis and King, the Australian explorers, starving.'

PULLMAN SLEEPING CARS *DUNROBIN* AND *BALMORAL* being hauled to Grosvenor Road, 1921. From 1885 to 1907, these cars were part of the Inverness to Glasgow night train. They then lay forgotten at Brighton, until brought to Seaford and, minus wheels, set on concrete foundations and incorporated into a house for Mr Marks. Interior doors and marquetry panels (with an owl motif) were retained till the house was demolished in 1977.

FROWD'S MILK LORRY overturned on the corner of Sutton Road and Warwick Road. Mr C.S. Frowd's shop was at 32 Broad Street. In the background is Pigeon House, recalling the days when this area was farmland. The building has changed little since this photograph was taken; the balcony railings were removed when the house was divided into flats.

VIEW FROM GUTTED PROJECTION ROOM, EMPIRE CINEMA, February 1939. Though Newhaven fire engine took only seven minutes to reach the scene – driven so furiously that the manifold burned out and had to be held together on the return journey – nothing could save the building. Fireman Mace lost his life when the escape, being used as a water tower, was blown to the ground. The Sutton Road site remains empty.

MRS WINSER'S CORONATION PARTY, Vale Road, June 1953. No doubt many mature Seaforders will recognize their young selves, well wrapped up against an English summer's day, at this celebration given by Mrs Winser (extreme right), Mrs Pook (on left in dark coat) and other parents.

THE GRANT OF ARMS, CROUCH HOUSE, 1953, to Seaford Urban District Council. 'Argent on water carry wavy a lymphad sailing to the sinister proper pennons flying gules a chief per pale of the last and or thereon to the dexter two demi lions passant guardant gold conjoined with as many sterns of ships of the field in pale and to the sinister an eagle displayed sable.' Within twenty-one years the arms were redundant, when Seaford became part of Lewes District.

CUTTING THROUGH HAWTH HILL to make the Buckle by-pass, 1963. Until the town had this alternative route, the usual way between Seaford and Newhaven was along the coast road past the Buckle Inn. When rough seas made that impassable, the landlord could activate an illuminated sign near the thatched hut in the foreground, advising drivers to go via Hill Rise, Grand Avenue and Firle Road.

FIRE AT CHAMPION'S RADIO WORKS, STEYNE ROAD, 1951. The factory stood on the west corner of The Causeway. It was wrecked by the fire and never used again.

Schools

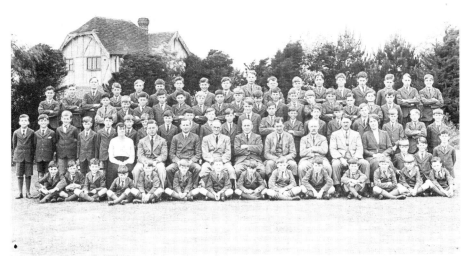

SEAFORD AS AN EDUCATIONAL CENTRE. From the late nineteenth century, boarding schools were attracted to this part of the coast by the fine air and quiet surroundings, and by the extensive sites available for establishing purpose-built premises. By the outbreak of the Second World War in 1939, Seaford was said to be 'ringed with an almost continuous green belt of school playing fields.'

RIDING AT SEAFORD LADIES' COLLEGE, EASTBOURNE ROAD, 1920. Miss H.M. Comfort came to Seaford from Beckley and established her college in seafront premises, but some six years later moved to new buildings on the outskirts of the town. With Miss Paine, she developed a renowned girls' school that lasted for over fifty years. Now called East Quinton, it is a County Council special school.

ONE OF THE SCHOOLROOMS AT ANNECY, SUTTON AVENUE. The sisters came to Seaford from France at the turn of the century, and their first pupils, some thirty boarders aged between ten and sixteen, were also drawn from both sides of the Channel. In more modern times, a number of showbusiness personalities, including Penelope Keith, Dickie Henderson and his twin sisters, and Terence Morgan were educated here.

STEYNE ROAD NATIONAL SCHOOL at the turn of the century. The teacher is Miss Agnes Mary Vernham. The school opened on 2 March 1859, the foundation stone having been laid by John Purcell FitzGerald the previous year. He had headed the subscription list, and served on the first management committee. Boys and girls attended here at first, but by 1879 a separate school for girls had been built in Church Street.

OUTING TO BEXHILL LEAVING CHURCH STREET SCHOOL, around 1900. The foot of the steps to the church west door is on the left, and the boundary wall and corner of the flint-built school on the right. The brick ladder-pattern is there to this day, but the gateway has been moved. The building marked 'Creamery' and others in the top left-hand corner survived two World Wars before becoming part of the present post office site.

LADYCROSS SCHOOL FROM THE DINGLE. In 1909 Mr A.F. Roper brought the school from Bournemouth to a fifteen-acre site fronting Eastbourne Road. The Lower School extension (on the right, known as 'the zoo') was added in 1927. Ladycross became one of the leading Roman Catholic boys' schools in the country. It was sold in 1977 and later demolished; Ladycross Close is one of the residential roads now occupying the site.

ST PETER'S SCHOOL CHAPEL. When the school was closed and the contents auctioned in 1982, prior to demolition and re-development as Bromley Road and its culs-de-sac, several items from the chapel came to Seaford Museum. Only a few months before, a former pupil of the school had distinguished himself in the Falklands War. He was Colonel 'H' Jones, posthumously awarded the Victoria Cross.

SEAFORD GIRLS' STOOLBALL TEAM, 1921. This ancient Sussex game is traditionally believed to have been invented by milkmaids. A popular revival followed the First World War, when it was used as a convalescent aid for wounded ex-servicemen. Back row, left to right: Ethel Templeman, Florence Simmons, Grace Styles, Ivy Matthews, Laura Osborne. Middle row, left to right: Betty Pettitt, Maisie Ward, Miss Pollard (umpire), Lydia Cheal. Seated, left to right: Gwen Pegler, May Simmons, Eileen Lucas.

SEAFORD GIRLS' NETBALL TEAM, 1930/31. Posing in the playground behind Church Street school, these girls were runners-up in the East Sussex Schools Netball League. Kindly identified by Miss Rose Fears, they include Gladys Horne, Edna Banks, Miss Gladham (umpire), Violet Cosstick, and Rose Fears herself.

KINGSLEIGH SCHOOL FOR GIRLS, SUTTON AVENUE, around 1934. At this time, the headmistress was Miss Worskett. By 1951 the building was used as a convalescent home for the Furnishing Trades Benevolent Association. Modernized, extended and re-named Whiteley House, in the 1970s it was acquired as extra accommodation for Micklefield School.

NORMANSAL SCHOOL, FIRLE ROAD. Normansal was founded in 1929 in an updated existing school building, and extended five years later to double its capacity; more accommodation was added when required. Besides academic subjects, the boys were encouraged in music, drama, carpentry and handicrafts, and latterly had their own printing press. Golf, volleyball and badminton were offered in addition to the more usual sports, and they had a heated indoor swimming pool. The premises are now called Chalvington.

HARVEST FESTIVAL, 1958, at Chyngton Primary School, Millberg Road, corner of Saltwood Road. The school was opened on 21 April 1958 to accommodate children from the Golden Key and other post-war developments on former farmland on the eastern side of Seaford. Church Street school had until then been the only local authority primary school in the town. Note the harvest message cut into the giant marrow borne by the boy third from right.

SECTION FOURTEEN

Military

MEN OF THE TERRITORIAL ARMY, No. 1 (210 Seaford) Squadron Royal Engineers, outside the Queen's Hall, Broad Street, 1938/9. These pre-war 'Saturday night soldiers' proved their worth at the outbreak of the Second World War. In May 1959, the 'Two-Ten' was presented with a sword of freedom (which is now displayed at the Downs Centre) and exercised its newly-conferred right to march through the town with fixed bayonets.

BLATCHINGTON BATTERY, 1870. The battery was built with ten cannon in 1761, on rising ground known as Blatchington Down, to the west of today's Salts Recreation Ground. Thirty-three years later a barracks was added when invasion from France was anticipated, and the mutiny of the Oxfordshire Militia in 1795 began here. Though it continued to be manned until its demolition, it no longer had a belligerent role; the master gunner even ran a small school there. In the 1880s, the land was sold for the Queen's Park estate.

RECREATION TENT, run by the Young Men's Christian Association. Seaford was a popular venue for summer manoeuvres from the turn of the century. Major Crook of Telsemaure annually invited the Honourable Artillery Company, and many were the parades, balls, mock battles and general high jinks witnessed by the locals. Boys earned pocket money by retrieving cannonballs from the earth bank used for target practice. In both World Wars, many troops camped in the area.

SOUTH CAMP CINEMA, 1914-?-18. Two vast camps were built to accommodate all the troops who passed through the area, either in training or *en route* across the Channel to the Western Front. North Camp was in the Blatchington area, and South Camp towards Chyngton. After the Armistice many of the huts were sold off, and a few are still in use around the town and elsewhere.

HOME GUARD PARADE, BROAD STREET. During the Second World War the Local Defence Volunteers were formed, later renamed Home Guard, though popularly known fifty years later as 'Dad's Army'. Its ranks were indeed filled by men too old for active service, or too young. Like the militia in barracks and Martello towers a century and a half before, they awaited a cross-Channel invasion that never came.

PRESENTATION EVENING AT THE QUEEN'S HALL, BROAD STREET. The boys are members of No. 2 Independent (Seaford) Cadet Troop, Royal Engineers, Sussex Army Cadet Force.

Storms, Floods and Wrecks

SOME TWO HUNDRED SHIPS are known to have come to grief in Seaford Bay; sea-bed relics dating from early times suggest many more unrecorded. Atlantic gales, cross-currents and sudden fogs were always natural hazards; for centuries, the locals were likened to scavenging birds for their evil practice of picking over washed-up cargoes and corpses from wrecks they caused by changing navigation lights on shore. 'God save us from the Seaford shags' was the sailors' prayer.

STEYNE ROAD after the Great Flood of 1875. West House (above) was occupied by Mr Bull's Academy for Gentlemen; the school was evacuated to Place House, Broad Street. One teacher who left a graphic account of the disaster was Hermann Ebbinghaus, who later pioneered psychology. Flood-water filled the ground-floor rooms to the ceilings; with such force did it rush through that fire-surrounds were dislodged and paper stripped from the walls. Marine Terrace (below) suffered likewise, with water filling the cellars. The *Sussex Advertiser* reported damage to forty-nine houses and '42 poor families who had lost nearly all their little furniture and clothes.'

AFTER THE FLOOD: Steyne Road (now Nos 49 and 51). Hurricane-force winds swept the country and the south coast in particular, causing the sea opposite Steyne Road (the ancient 'Quayside') to burst through the protective shingle bank in three places, pouring into the nearest houses. 'The greatest difficulty is to get things dry again, because the salt won't go out and all the water about here is brackish, therefore we cannot wash it out,' wrote Ebbinghaus.

LIFESAVERS AT THE BUCKLE, 1913. The number of ships in difficulty in Seaford Bay over the centuries has prompted the formation of a variety of rescue services. The Newhaven lifeboat and the Coastguard service (of which Richard Mallett is perhaps our best known member) have saved many lives. The group shown here had members of several old Seaford families, including Simmons, Kneller and Templeman.

DANISH BARQUE *PERUVIAN* aground opposite the Esplanade Hotel, February 1899. Net tonnage 591, with a cargo of logwood and vegetable ivory, she came ashore in heavy seas. Ten of the eleven crew were saved. Unloading the cargo began, then fresh gales smashed her against the sea-wall and sparks flew, witnessed by many sightseers. Her figurehead, one cat-head and some 'ivory nuts' are displayed in Seaford Museum.

BELGIAN STEAMER *COMTESSE DE FLANDRE* aground at the foot of Crowlink, 30 December 1925. This event made headlines in the national newspapers next day. The *Daily Mail* reported how the twenty-seven-man crew was saved, and carried dramatic photographs of the breeches-buoy rescue from the clifftop. Several other ships have been wrecked or beached at this spot over the centuries, notably the *Nympha Americana* in 1747.

FLOODED COAST ROAD AT THE BUCKLE, 1913. Although the building of Claremont Road in 1879 saved travellers from some of the hazards of the old, eroded coastal route to Newhaven, they had still to brave the exposed corner near the Buckle Inn, where the sea was only yards away. Local Royal Academician Sir Frank Short made a well-known sketch of a Southdown bus (single-decker) splashing through. It was another fifty years before a by-pass was built.

STEYNE ROAD FLOOD, 1949. Little maintenance had been possible on the sea-wall during the Second World War, and flooding like this resulted until a programme of major works could be carried out. Here Mr Sam Simmons, of the ancient family of longshoremen, rows his boat in strange waters.

THE *WALTER RICHTER* AGROUND AT TIDEMILLS, February 1972. The 430-ton German coaster with a cargo of beechwood drove ashore in a gale. Emergency services and members of the public set up the breeches-buoy apparatus by which the crew of six was saved. Repeated efforts by German tugs *Danzig* and *Hermes* failed to move her. After a month, during which the tide-battered vessel became a tourist attraction, Newhaven tugs *Meeching* and *Mallard*, working with a shore-based winch, freed her.

Panoramas

LOOKING WEST TOWARDS TIDEMILLS, around 1870. This is the earliest known photograph of the seafront, and gives a clear impression of the low-lying area behind the shingle bank, where the River Ouse once flowed. Indeed, a vestigial stream, complete with bridge, can be seen below the Martello Tower hillock. In the centre is Seaford Battery, reduced to rubble by the 1875 flood. The house with low buildings behind is Telsemaure.

VIEW ACROSS THE COMMON TO THE STEYNE, before 1875. On the extreme left is the workshop of Ockenden, the wheelright, on the corner of Church Street. This wooden building was totally wrecked by the flood of 14 November 1875. In the cottage next door lived an elderly man who was rescued by boat from an upstairs window, in the same disaster. The open common in the foreground is today occupied by the Methodist church and part of the Admiral's Walk development.

ACROSS THE COMMON TO THE STEYNE AND LEACH'S LANE (CROUCH LANE). Still with us are the Tudor cannon on the corner, and the flint wall and gateway of Seaford House, for a short time the home of Poet Laureate, Alfred Lord Tennyson. A third building of the same name now occupies the site.

SEAFORD FROM THE NORTH EAST. The original is marked 'Kite photograph over 300 feet.' Running across the centre is East Street/Warwick Road, crossing the old and new ways towards Eastbourne – Sutton Road in the middle and Sutton Park Road to the right. On the extreme right is the south-west corner of the old 'cats' cemetery' plot of rough ground, the site of the War Memorial since 1952. The church tower is on the left near the skyline; to the right and slightly down, the large dark house is Place House, built in 1603 for the Gratwicke family, on the corner of Broad Street and Place Lane.

FROM THE ESPLANADE HOTEL LOOKING NORTH EAST, 1949. Running across the middle of this snapshot, Steyne Road can be readily identified, with West House on the left, past Parliament Row and Alexandra Terrace to Marine Terrace on the right. Most of the foreground area has since been developed but the building with the high round window remains, now the Little Theatre.

FROM THE PARISH CHURCH LOOKING SOUTH, 1949. Running down from the seafront are (left to right) Ringmer Road, the Causeway, St John's Road and West View, with boarding-houses and hotels including the prestigious Esplanade. In the foreground are the open spaces left by the bombing of Church Street, Pinders Square and West Street, now occupied by the police station and car park.

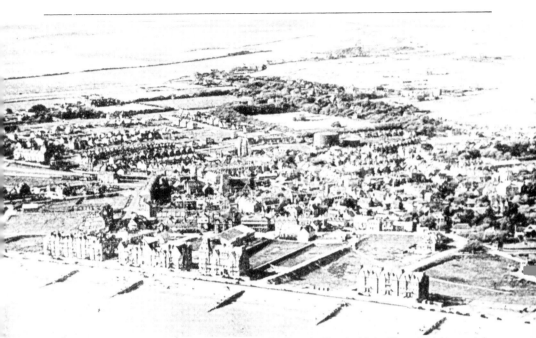

AERIAL VIEW FROM THE SOUTH EAST, 1930s. The Esplanade Hotel with its French château-style tower dominated the seafront from 1894 for some seventy years; the site has now been developed as Mallett Close, with further building land available. Prominent in this photograph are the causeways linking the seafront and Steyne Road, put in by early developers who left without building the rows of boarding-houses envisaged. The tall buildings in the centre were part of the old gasworks; the gasometer was added in 1912.

LOOKING NORTH EAST FROM SUTTON MILL, towards Hindover and Alfriston. The mill is believed to date from 1769, the date recorded on a piece of oak found when dismantling the buildings in 1904. The millhouse remains to this day, and relics of the windmill, such as the grindstones, have been incorporated in houses built on the site.

VIEW OF CHURCH STREET LOOKING NORTH, near the junction with Dane Road (left) and Clinton Place (right). From the parish church tower, the photographer had a privileged view into the back gardens of Nos 1, 2 and 3 Gloster Place. The curved wall in the middle marked the boundary of the railway land, and Claremont Road can be seen leading away to the left at the top of the picture.

Tidemills

THE GRANARY OF TIDEMILLS, with some of the workers' cottages, from the south west, 1883. An Act of Parliament in 1761 permitted the building of a mill across the creek which was all that remained of the old tidal river running east towards Seaford. Fifty years later, under William Catt's management, the mill was working sixteen hours a day and producing 1,500 sacks of flour per week.

TIDEMILLS GRANARY AND COTTAGES with south millpond, 1883. At the height of its productivity, there were some sixty workers at Tidemills, most of whom lived in the village with their families. After it closed, employees of the Harbour Company occupied the cottages, which later were used as holiday homes, and part of Mr Dale's stables. The village had its own railway halt; the platforms remain, though it closed in 1942.

TIDEMILLS FROM THE EAST. As well as his success as a miller, William Catt was renowned for his gardening projects. The large millhouse, in the centre of this picture, had pear trees growing on its west-facing wall, fastened espalier-style. Grapes grew successfully in the glasshouse on the right. William drained much of the surrounding marshland and made fertile farmland, cultivated to this day.

TIDEMILLS COTTAGES, 1936. Some eighty years earlier the village had featured in Charles Dickens's *Household Words*, when the writer attempted to buy 'Oysters fresh from the beds' as advertised at Holter's House. His attention was drawn to the rest of the notice, 'Sundays excepted', and he went away hungry.

RUINS OF TIDEMILLS, LOOKING EAST, 1969. At the beginning of the Second World War, the remaining villagers were evacuated, together with patients and staff from the Marine Hospital. The cottages and all other buildings were demolished, and today only a few pieces of flint wall are left to tell the tale of a once-thriving community. In-filling, vandalism and the ravages of time and weather have hastened the process.

MARINE HOSPITAL, TIDEMILLS, around 1935. The young patients at this branch of Chailey Heritage are staging their own Boat Race, in spite of their disabilities. Most boys were crippled with polio or rickets, or had suffered amputations. Playing in the sea and breathing the strong sea air were part of their rehabilitation.

Nearby

LITLINGTON PLEASURE GARDENS. Established more than seventy years ago by Mr Russell as a popular venue for picnics and other excursions, the nursery and tea gardens, with rare plants and novelties, have continued to be patronized by locals and visitors, including royalty. A guidebook of 1937 dismissed Litlington as 'where the staple industry is making tea and cutting bread and butter' . . . and why not?

THE WHITE HORSE UNDER HINDOVER HILL, from the Cuckmere. Tradition has it that the horse, almost ninety feet long, was cut in one night by three men in 1924. They were led by John Ade, whose ancestor William had helped to create a similar animal many years before on the same hillside. The second horse was camouflaged during the Second World War, but restored soon after.

THE CUCKMERE FROM HINDOVER HILL. The white horse lies immediately below the flowering bushes, on the hillside. The river meanders towards Alfriston, the route taken by many an illicit cargo smuggled ashore at the haven.

BLATCHINGTON STREET, 1931, looking to Belgrave Road crossing. The pillars on the left mark the entrance to Blatchington Court, though today the drive leads nowhere, as the school has been demolished to make way for Clarke's development. Opposite, all creeper has now gone from the flint walls of The Gables. Like the village street of Bishopstone, this part of Blatchington Hill has seen little change in the last seventy years.

BLATCHINGTON PRIVATE RESIDENTIAL HOTEL. The former Arlington House was built in around 1800 as a family home in three acres of ground. In the twentieth century it served as a hotel till 1954, when it was acquired as a retirement home by the Civil Service Benevolent Fund and renamed Blatchington House.

THE CUCKMERE AT ALFRISTON, 1907, looking south. From the fourteenth-century church of St Andrew across the river bridge, a path leads up a steep slope to the tiny church (in fact, a surviving chancel) at Lullington. This route follows the South Downs Way.

ALFRISTON MARKET CROSS. One of only two such crosses left in Sussex (the other is in Chichester), it stands in tiny Waterloo Square as a symbol of Alfriston's antiquity. The village appeared in Domesday as Alvricestone. In the early nineteenth century, it was the operational centre for the infamous activities of smuggler Stanton Collins and his gang.

THE TEA-COURT AT DRUSILLA'S, ALFRISTON. Sent on 13 April 1932, this postcard exactly conveys the spirit of the times, though one wonders how many silk stockings were snagged on those cumbersome basket chairs. From its original conception as a tea-shop and catering school, Drusilla's has developed in some seventy years into a twenty-acre playpark with railway and zoo featuring penguins, monkeys and meerkats.

Birling Farm and Downs.

BIRLING FARM looking east, 1907. 'Do you know this?' That remains a good question: considerable detective work among Seaford Museum files was needed to decide that the building at the foot of the steep slope, since altered and enlarged, is now called The Shepherd's Cottage, dating from around 1860. The road to Birling Gap runs through the trees to the right. The farmhouse is known today as Birling Manor.

985

THE LONG MAN OF WILMINGTON, EASTBOURNE

THE WILMINGTON GIANT. Some 230 ft tall, the Long Man confronts us from the northern slope of Windover Hill. Theories as to his origins are as many as interpretations of his significance. Nobody knows for sure, but all agree that his importance to historians and tourists alike warrants every care for his preservation.